The Case for a Royal Commission on the Penal System

Sir Louis Blom-Cooper

Seán McConville

Foreword by Sir Henry Brooke

November 2014

Queen Mary
University of London
School of Law

WATERSIDE PRESS

The Case for a Royal Commission on the Penal System

ISBN 978-1-909976-17-7 (Paperback)

ISBN 978-1-908162-88-5 (EPUB ebook)

ISBN 978-1-908162-89-2 (Adobe ebook)

Cataloguing-In-Publication Data

A catalogue record for this booklet can be obtained on request from the British Library.

Cover design by www.gibgob.com © Waterside Press.

UK distributor Gardners Books, 1 Whittle Drive, Eastbourne, East Sussex, BN23 6QH.
Tel: +44 (0)1323 521777; sales@gardners.com; www.gardners.com

North American distributor Ingram Book Company, One Ingram Blvd, La Vergne, TN 37086, USA.
Tel: (+1) 615 793 5000; inquiry@ingramcontent.com

Published by
Waterside Press Ltd.
Sherfield Gables
Sherfield on Loddon
Hook, Hampshire
United Kingdon RG27 0JG

Telephone +44(0)1256 882250
E-mail enquiries@watersidepress.co.uk
Online catalogue WatersidePress.co.uk

Contents

Foreword

Sir Henry Brooke

When I was a sentencing judge I was interested in trying to learn more about the effect of the sentences I imposed. If I made a probation order, I would direct that I should receive quarterly reports on progress. This served two purposes—to acquaint myself with the value (or otherwise) of what I was doing, and to let the probation officer and the offender know that the sentencing judge was keeping an eye on the outcome of what he had done.

For much the same reason if my court list outside London collapsed, as it very often did, I would make arrangements to visit a local prison or young offender institution, or go to a local probation day centre, in order to get a better idea of the effect of different sentencing choices. It would have been good if it had also been possible to receive well-informed feedback on the eventual outcome of the custodial and other community sentences I passed.

It was, I believe, the same kind of intellectual curiosity that impelled my father to set up the Royal Commission on the Penal System 50 years ago, soon after he was appointed Home Secretary. I happened to be living at home at the time, and I remember his concern (as befitted a Balliol philosophy don manqué) about the absence of any really coherent up-to-date thinking within Government about the purposes of penal policy.

The rack, the stocks, the pillory, the ducking-stool, the treadmill, the convict ships and segregation in silence had long since passed into history. Corporal punishment was outlawed in 1948 and capital punishment was on its way out, as the unfair inconsistencies inherent in the compromise Homicide Act 1957 became more and more apparent. Community service orders were a thing of the future: for adult offenders without mental health problems, fines, probation orders and discharges (absolute or conditional) were the only non-custodial options. So far as custodial sentences were concerned, it was an important part of Home Office thinking at that time that imprisonment for ten years or more caused a man or woman to become institutionalised, with little hope of living a constructive self-sufficient life thereafter. Perhaps it was for this reason there had been no new prison-building for adults for more than 50 years: long-term incarceration was not thought to be a very good idea.

As things turned out that Commission was wound up two years later, its remit unfulfilled. Whether it was the inordinate breadth of its terms of reference, the chemistry of the relationships between some of the strong-minded commissioners and the chairman's inability to control them, or the fact that the incoming Wilson Government had its own ideas about penal policy which it wanted to implement immediately without waiting for the Commission, are matters for historians to argue about. What is beyond doubt is that since 1966—and particularly since 1992—penal policy has developed in fits and starts, with Ministers blown about by the occasional gust of public outrage, enthusiastically fanned by circulation-seeking tabloids. Authoritative, truly independent advisory bodies are seen by our rulers today as yesterday's way of doing things. The result has been a fairly expensive disaster. A spell of quiet, constructive independent-minded thinking is needed. The situation needs it, and the public deserve it.

When Sir Louis first asked me to write this foreword, my response was fairly defeatist. I remembered talks given 15 years ago to the criminal justice NGO I used to chair by a senior Home Office researcher and a newly appointed, lateral-thinking Home Office junior Minister. They described, explicitly or implicitly, a Jekyll and Hyde scenario in the Home Office. On the one hand there was the thoughtful development of penal policy founded on an increasing volume of evidence-based research. On the other hand there was the influence of massive publicity given by the tabloids to the victims of individual hard cases and the mantra in sub-editors' headlines which proclaimed that this or that offender 'walked free' even though he or she had been given a demanding community sentence. Readers were presumed not to know that this would stretch the offender far more effectively than a spell of degrading incarceration with little to fill the time except to feel sorry for oneself, resolve to avoid being caught next time, and learn from fellow inmates the best techniques for achieving this desired end.

I happened to be a sentencing judge at the time the political tide turned in 1992 when a newly re-elected government was listening far more intently to its PR advisers than to the counsel of those who really understood 'what worked' and 'what didn't work' in terms of the treatment of offenders. The emasculation of the thoughtful Criminal Justice Act 1991 and its substitution by the 'prison works' philosophy so vividly articulated by Michael Howard led to a major shift of resources away from the constructive use of prisoners' time to the building of more and more prison places, staffed by prison officers who were increasingly less experienced as their numbers grew and grew, and the diversion of funds away from educational and workshop resources to meeting the cost of incarcerating more and more prisoners, with far more emphasis being placed now on security than on rehabilitation.

One particular memory says it all. I visited Feltham Young Offender Institution twice during a three-year period during those years. On the first occasion I saw a new toy-making workshop in which young offenders were being taught to deploy their creative skills, and also a National Association for the Care and Resettlement of Offenders (now Nacro) unit where efforts were being made to find post-release placements which did not simply mean that the offender went back to the street culture which was his natural pre-conviction habitat. I remember emerging from Feltham that day with two teddy bears I had purchased at the workshop: they later found their way to a children's charity in Bosnia. There was a feeling of hope among the senior staff at Feltham that their efforts were starting to make a difference. When I returned in 1997, the workshop had closed. The Nacro unit had closed. Hope had turned to despair. And the chief inspector's observation that teenagers who had not reached the compulsory school leaving age were not receiving any lessons at all had led not to the provision of greater educational resources but to the switching of such resources as survived the cuts from teaching the teachable to teaching the virtually unteachable.

As I write, both Jekyll and Hyde are still hard at work. Dr Jekyll is taking unprecedented steps to elevate the importance of rehabilitation if the crime rate is to be cut. Mr Hyde is making that goal far, far harder to attain by driving forward policies that may leave the huge prison population locked up for longer than ever, particularly at weekends; doing little or nothing to reduce its size; increasing prisoners' frustration by removing their access to trusted means of redress for justified complaints; and encouraging the employment of cheaper and inevitably less experienced prison staff. Though some very good things are being done, the implementation of Lord Justice Woolf's recommendations, which followed some very serious prison riots and an in-depth study of international best practice, seems to be further away than ever.

All these thoughts led me to change my mind and say 'yes' to Sir Louis' request. We cannot as a nation go on as we are. Fresh thinking is needed about the purposes of penal policy in the 21st-century. A well-composed Royal Commission, with tightly drawn terms of reference and a sensibly time-limited mandate, would provide guidance to the better way forward we should all be seeking. It would be a wonderful thing if all our major political parties were to agree that the period after the next General Election should provide the thinking time in which such a Commission could inspire a well-informed debate about the purposes of punishment and the best ways of achieving those purposes. Perhaps I might see my father's unfinished business completed in my own lifetime, as even the dissentient members of his own Commission so clearly hoped.

If Not Now, When?

Sir Louis Blom-Cooper

I. Introduction

Penology and the English prison system have been passionate interests ever since I read the trenchant argument in the report of the Royal Commission on Capital Punishment (1949-1953). This outstanding Blue Book was sadly neglected thereafter in official circles save for abolition of the death penalty in 1965. But that crucial issue was excluded from its terms of reference, although it impliedly indicated it as the only alternative. It was the pronouncements of Sir Ernest Gowers and his colleagues in 1953 that nevertheless prompted my impetus to play a minor role in the nascent campaign for the abolition of capital punishment. Ruth Ellis' execution in 1955 was a disgraceful exercise of the prerogative power of mercy that led inexorably to abolition in 1965. Following the aborted dissolution of the Royal Commission on the Penal System (1964-1966) I was appointed by the Home Secretary, Roy Jenkins, as a member of the Advisory Council on the Penal System (1966-1978). Since its demise in 1980 I have kept a weather-eye on the all too frequently depressing state of the English prison system. I became the chairman of the Howard League for Penal Reform (1973-1984) and was a founder member of the Prison Reform Trust in 1981. In recent years I followed the diminishing number of countries that outlawed the uncivilised practice of executing their citizens as a retribution for unjustified homicide; this development is graphically told in the various issues of *The Death Penalty* internationally edited by Professors Roger Hood and Carolyn Hoyle at Oxford University for the United Nations. Keeping this keen watch on developments I am ever more aware of the frustration and dissatisfaction that have been building-up about the purpose, structure and functioning of the penal system. The time is more than ripe for an official study and review.

When six members of the Royal Commission on the Penal System wrote in January 1965 to the (incoming) Labour Home Secretary, foreshadowing their resignation and the ultimate unprecedented dissolution of the Royal Commission in April 1966, they said the following:

> '…we believe that a period of active major legislation[1] is not an opportune one for conducting the kind of assessment and philosophical appreciation envisaged in our terms of reference. We believe, however, that a Royal Commission set up some years hence would be of great service.'

Half a century on we think that a 'great service' would indeed be afforded by the establishing of a Royal Commission on Penal Affairs, and over the last two decades have urged that this be done. In a letter carried by *The Times* on the centenary (April 1995) of the submission to the Home Secretary, Herbert Asquith, of the recommendations of a landmark Departmental Report on Prisons of 1895, under the chairmanship of Herbert Gladstone, it was stressed that that committee advocated explicit adoption of the philosophies of deterrence and rehabilitation. These twin aims of deterrence and rehabilitation came to dominate penal policy and the practice of penal philosophies for much of the 20th-century. By the last decades of the 20th-century, questions about deterrence and retribution had acquired currency and indeed urgency, as indeed had their relationship. Rehabilitation has recently been revived by the Coalition Government as a penal policy, in the form of a renewed drive to break the circle of constant re-offending.

The Times letter which is reproduced in *Appendix II* hereto was signed by no fewer than eleven prominent citizens, including the then Archbishop of Canterbury (Lord Runcie); the chairman of the Parole Board at its inception in 1967 (Lord Hunt); a former Home Secretary from 1967-1970 and Prime Minister (Lord Callaghan); the Permanent Secretary of the Home Office from 1966-1972 (Lord Allen of Abbeydale) and other persons of distinction and experience in public life.

In a subsequent letter advocating a review of the penal system the signatories were joined by Douglas Hurd (now Lord Hurd of Westwell), Home Secretary 1985-1989. He was joined by Martin Narey, former Director General of the Prison

---

1. They were referring to the Labour Administration's Bill on Criminal Justice which followed from the Party's report in the early-1960s (the Alice Bacon report).

Service and as Permanent Under Secretary at the Home Office prominent in the establishment of NOMS (the National Offender Management Service) and by Lord Woolf, then a retired Lord Chief Justice (again, see *Appendix II* where further letters are also reproduced). We think that it is more than just appropriate that persons of such great and detailed experience and public rectitude in penal matters should append their signatures to a letter calling for an independent review of penal policy for the 21st-century.

The present state of our prison system, as chronicled in penetrating reports from successive chief inspectors of prisons—from Judge Stephen Tumim, Lord Ramsbotham, Dame Anne Owers and Mr Nick Hardwick—is such as to cause confusion in the minds of many members of the public, and even among the administrators and operators of the Prison Service (particularly at a time when the daily average prison population has escalated alarmingly over recent years). The very valuable recommendations of the 1990/1991 inquiry into prison disturbances by Lord (then Lord Justice) Woolf proposed a civilised regime for prisons, and justice for prisoners, but these objectives have now, to some extent, been overtaken by other agendas. Lord Woolf's inquiry did not have a remit to consider related and important aspects of sentencing policy (see below) and practice. The discredited and essentially empty political rhetoric, current since the mid-1990s, of being 'tough on crime and tough on the causes of crime', has been substantially replaced by a tough approach, 'intelligently informed'.

From the time of the Second World War, the signatories of *The Times* correspondence observed, and for some four decades, successive administrations relied heavily on advice from independent committees on penal matters. From 1980 onwards (but more particularly after the passing of the useful Criminal Justice Act 1991) there has been, quite deliberately, a refusal by Government to countenance any independent corporate (meaning collective and disparate) advice; indeed a parliamentary attempt by the House of Lords in 1998 to revive the Advisory Council on the Penal System was specifically rejected by the Home Secretary, Jack Straw. Doubtless they saw such advice, once given currency, as inhibiting their own policy choices and indeed their often politically useful rhetoric.

Policy on the twin problems of crime and punishment is hopelessly confused, confounded by the current stream of this rhetoric. The broad consensus on crime policy of the post-Second World War decades has been abandoned. Instead, battle lines are daily reinforced in the destructive conflict between hardliners and even those who strive to present themselves as harderliners, and those who advocate principles of restoration within criminal justice. It is our contention that these shifts and conflicts are contrary to the national interest, and will contribute to increased division and social deterioration.

Police services are nowadays less than well-regarded by the average citizen. The courts have come under increasing criticism for assumed leniency towards offenders and their failure to control a supposedly inexorable rise in crime — even though crime has apparently been on a steady downward trend for some years. The judiciary is publicly at odds with the Secretary of State for Justice over sentencing policy, with almost annual Criminal Justice Acts. There is an unprecedented slump in morale within the Prison Service (not always evident in media reports), whose members feel incapable of meeting the conflicting demands of the public to contain and deter criminals, to run a humane system of containment, and yet cope with the largest recorded prison population, all with severely constrained finances.

Security and public order are the prime tasks of government. These tasks are not assisted by the present nature of criminal justice, which is neither a unitary, nor even a unified system. The various parts of that system — police, prosecution, courts, probation and prison services — often address quite different agendas.

All the different agencies in the criminal process are now subject to being measured, either at the behest of the Audit Commission or the National Audit Office. The various inspectorates (now combined under one umbrella), and the national objectives enunciated by the Home Office and later the Ministry of Justice, also place increased emphasis on measurement and quality control (altogether more difficult to assess). Yet none of these evaluations takes account of the impact of the agencies, each on the other. There is an urgent need to coalesce the parts of the criminal process, to make them parts of a more functional machinery. The increasing privatisation of penal administration and its effect on policy needs a more strategic consideration. And there is another area for examination: what part should the civil process play in support of criminal justice?

Criminal justice itself is probably marginal to the problem of crime control, but, when its overall tasks are improperly or inadequately addressed, the quality of the citizen's life sharply declines. The means of achieving order, of controlling crime at a tolerable level and of imposing just and effective punishments are many and complicated, and certainly do not lie in the hands of Government alone. The notion of a civilised society—a community at ease with itself—embraces its cultural, economic and technological achievements, but also that blend of liberty, security and community which is the foundation of civic contentment.

In short, the time is more than apt for a Royal Commission, to assess and restate the modern philosophical purposes of penal affairs, and more specifically to enunciate the purpose of imprisonment as a social response to crime.

II. Independent Corporate Advice on Penal Affairs

Looking at the reports of review and advice issued by independent bodies, we think that it becomes clear that only parts of penal policy and administration have thus been investigated. Indeed there have been topics of importance to penal policy-makers and administrators that have been dealt with without the benefit of independent corporate advice. The privatising of the bulk of the Probation Service in April 2014 is a prime example of untested penal policy.

After the Second World War the Home Secretary set up a standing committee to examine such aspects of the law as he might refer to it, to consider whether the criminal law and procedure required revision, and to make recommendations. The committee which followed the Departmental Committee on Mentally Abnormal Offenders was composed exclusively of judges and lawyers (practitioners, administrators and academics). It overlapped with the other advisory councils to the extent of examining on five occasions the penalty for murder, following the abolition of capital punishment in 1965 and its confirmation in December 1969, and reference to all offences against the person by the Home Secretary in March 1970. Only the Advisory Council on the Penal System, in its report of 1978 on

Sentences of Imprisonment, considered the ending of the mandatory life sentence for murder. Otherwise, successive administrations have resolutely denied any intention to review the common law offence of murder, despite attempts, both official and voluntary, to urge the ending of the compulsory life sentence. This in turn involves the true relationship between Parliament and the Judicature since the passing of the Human Rights Act 1998.

The Criminal Law Revision Committee, which issued well over a dozen reports on aspects of the criminal law, unofficially survived until the mid-1980s, by which time it had been effectively superseded by the Law Commission, established in 1967 by the Labour administration. Its terms of reference, restricted to the ambit of the criminal law, nevertheless touched on aspects of the penal system.

Much of what goes on in the criminal courts affects penal administration; sentencing of offenders is linked to criminal responsibility and mental culpability. The movement towards recognition of the role and function of the victims of crime in the course of proceedings is shaping the procedure of the criminal courts, and trial by jury is the subject of public involvement in criminal justice. Modification of the mode of criminal trial for serious fraud offences is now actively being considered. Any review of the penal system must inevitably involve aspects of the criminal law.

A list of reports by the Advisory Council for the Treatment of Offenders (ACTO) and the Advisory Council on the Penal System (ACPS) appears in *Appendix I* hereto.

The terms of reference assigned to ACTO were 'to assist the Home Secretary with advice and suggestions on questions relating to the treatment of offenders'. The remit to the ACPS was significantly different; the terms of reference were covered by the more generic term of 'penal system', of which the treatment of offenders was only a part. The objective of 'prevention of crime' was also introduced. Professor Leon Radzinowicz, the doyen of academic criminology and the first director of the Institute of Criminology at Cambridge University, observed in his autobiographical book, *Adventures in Criminology*,[2] the reports 'represent an impressive record of inquiries into several central and consistently topical issues of criminal policy and the administration of criminal justice. It is no less remarkable that the recommendations of virtually all of them were adopted unanimously by the relevant sub-committee and the council as a whole'. Had the Royal Commission on the Penal System proceeded to report after 1966, it might have reflected on the utility of the topics covered by the two advisory bodies which enveloped either side of its incomplete deliberations.

A Government White Paper, *Crime, Justice and Protecting the Public* in 1990 stated:

> 'Nobody now regards imprisonment, in itself, as an effective means of reform for most prisoners … imprisonment … can be an expensive way of making bad people worse … most crimes are not violent … punishment in the community is likely to be better for the victims, public and offender'.

In 1992, Lord Woolf (later Lord Chief Justice) in his report on prison disturbances produced a programme of reform based on the primary need to balance security and justice. Imprisonment had always been a punishment of last resort, or had been for years; what changed in 1991 with the Criminal Justice Act of that year, based on the white paper, was that a statutory framework of commensurate sentencing was introduced, that later began to dissemble due to a mix of political and judicial manoeuvring. There were also considerable changes following Woolf.

Following this both main political parties adopted the rhetoric of 'tough on crime' (New Labour extending this to 'tough on crime, tough on the causes of crime'), which persisted for the next two decades. Criminal justice and penal affairs in legislative action and administrative decisions jettisoned humanity, proportionality and cost-effectiveness in the use of the prison estate: indeed these principles were substantially downplayed or even swept aside. Politics became the ominous order of the day. In October 2012, Prime Minister, David Cameron, in a rare speech on crime and justice, replaced the language with a 'tough and intelligent'

---

2.   London, Routledge, 1999, p 328.

formula. Any prospect of a follow-up of the 1990 declaration was seemingly still out of the question, although the language had ostensibly altered.

The Advisory Council on the Penal System had been established in June 1966 as the body designed to provide independent corporate advice to Ministers on specific issues of criminal justice and penal affairs. It was set up as a direct response to the unprecedentedly dissolved Royal Commission on the Penal System (1964-1966). The council survived until it was axed, along with many other quangos, by the Thatcher administration in 1980, since when no administration has desired to back independent corporate advice on any issues relating to crime and punishment. The council produced more than a dozen reports in its short life (the last being in June 1978), most of which reached the statute book. The continuing trend to illiberal decisions throughout the last 30 years has in large part been attributable to a denial of sensible reform and a deafening silence to penal affairs movement in Western Europe. Even attempts to revive an advisory body were stoutly resisted.

For 12 years (1966-1978) the Advisory Council's reports had formed an important strand in the formulation of policy. That was the conclusion of two academic commentators in 1979, writing in *Political Quarterly*.[3] In his book, *Responses to Crime*, Lord Windlesham, formerly a Home Office Minister (1971-2) and Parole Board Chairman (1982-1988), wrote:[4]

> 'In the ordinary way, no incoming Home Office minister, least of all one with the qualities and style of William Whitelaw, nor the officials advising him, would have contemplated abolishing the ACPS. Despite a recent hiccup, it was patently a body of good standing that had done valuable work. But the times were not ordinary. One of the earliest targets in the new Prime Minister's sights was the large cluster of non-departmental bodies which had proliferated during the years of consensus. In her scornful view many such bodies, known as quangos, were not simply unnecessary but represented an insidious spread

---

3. R Morgan and B Smith, 'Advising the Minister on Crime and Punishment', Vol. 50, No 3, pp 326-335.

4. *Responses to Crime*, Vol. III, Oxford: Oxford University Press, pp 148-149.

of patronage, concealing at the same time the growth that had taken place in the apparatus of central government. The growth, moreover, was one that was not disclosed in the statistics on the size of the Civil Service.

Even when in full flood the cost of the ACPS was modest. Neither the chairman nor members were paid any fees, the main expenditure being incurred in the preparation and publication of their reports. But what was the non-financial worth of its work? How did it measure up to the tests of being "essential" or "sufficiently valuable"? Most important of all in the minds of ministers and senior civil servants was the answer to the unspoken question: how should Whitehall react to the new broom at Number 10? … From the standpoint of the Home Secretary, and the Department as a whole, the priority was to preserve those bodies which were likely to be of the greatest utility.'

When the ACPS issued its last report in June 1978 on *Sentences of Imprisonment* it received an adverse reaction from academic commentators; it was never fully debated and despite the quality of its reasoning the report has not been independently reviewed. An academic commentator, Professor Rod Morgan, who became chairman of the Youth Justice Board (2004-2007), wrote in 1979 (before the dissolution of the APCS in 1980) that 'there can be no doubt about the importance of the issues with which it deals'. He added:

'The length of prison sentences, judicial discretion and provisions for the dangerous or exceptional offender are critical problems for future penal policy. Such issues raise difficult ethical, political and constitutional questions which are not likely to be solved within a single document. Even those who are critical of the recommendations advanced in the ACPS report may conclude that their publication might yet prove useful in precipitating an important and necessary public debate forcing individuals and groups who oppose their adoption to formulate acceptable policy alternatives. What we can say concerning the *Sentences of Imprisonment* report is that though it has been available for a year it has yet to lead to a serious public or parliamentary debate of the issues.'[5]

---

5.   Privately published.

In the three decades thereafter, the crucial subject of sentencing has been visited much, ultimately (in 2009) in a Sentencing Council which has usefully pronounced upon desirable sentence lengths imposed by sentencers, but based upon a spate of statutes which introduced a more and more complex system that judges found difficult to apply sensibly. The whole sentencing system needs a thorough revision, fortified by a consideration as to the philosophical underpinning to the vital question of punishment.

Since 1990, there have been several proposals that there should be established an independent, authoritative and authentic study of the penal system. The silence of successive governments, however, has been emphatic.

III. Aspects of the Penal System

(a) Penological problems

Of all the options available to the judges, Ministers of the Crown or to other prison administrators, identified by the last Lord Chief Justice, Lord Judge, in *R v Oakes and Others*[6] — namely punishment, deterrence, public protection or rehabilitation of the offender — Parliament should now indicate what options are available, and what order of priority each should be given. The statutes dealing with the disposal of offenders, both within and outwith the custodial system, have declined to indicate what penological options should be considered.

The Gladstone Committee of 1895 singled out deterrence and rehabilitation to replace the statutory system of separation in silence which had itself replaced the system operating since the middle of the 19th-century. Thereafter penal administrators operated upon a similar basis, although by the 1960s 'humane containment' (rather despairingly, and somewhat as a formula of last resort) had been adopted as the charter for penal regimes. Since then neither the Prison Service nor the system of sentencing has been sufficiently well-defined: that definition is urgently needed.

---

6.   [2012] EWCA Crim 2435.

(b) Sentencing

Of all the aspects of crime and punishment, the one that calls for immediate attention is the sentencing by the courts of offenders. Such is the urgency of review that the Law Commission in its *Eleventh Programme of Law Reform* on 19 July 2011 identified sentencing law as one of the projects considered for a study to simplify and consolidate all sentencing legislation (para 3.14, p 25 of HC 1407). The Lord Chancellor replied (p 26, para 3.21) that while he could *not* accept such a project 'at this time', nevertheless he had indicated that a project of this nature might be requested by the Government in the future. We heartily endorse this latter sentiment in advocating a review of sentencing law and practice post-May 2015; more specifically it must form part of our penal philosophy.

We would endorse the Law Commission's case for the project in paragraphs 3.15 to 3.17 and in particular cite the passage in the recent judgment of Lord Judge in *R (Noone) v Governor of Drake Hall Prison*.[7] He said on the subject of the spate of legislation:

'For too many years now the administration of criminal justice has been engulfed by a relentless tidal wave of legislation. The tide is always in flow: it has never ebbed … It is outrageous that so much intellectual effort, as well as public time and resources, have had to be expended in order to discover a route through the legislative morass to what should be, both for the prisoner herself, and for those responsible for her custody, the prison authorities, the simplest and most certain of questions — the prisoner's release date.

The Sentencing Council and the judiciary generally have shown their support for this project, with a view towards an overall assessment of the way in which sentencing should reflect the public's view to endorse its future policy towards punishment and its consequences for a civilised penal system.'

---

7.   [2010] UKSC 30, paras 80 and 87.

(c) Young offenders

It is 21 years since Robert Thompson and John Venables (both aged eleven) were sentenced to detention at Her Majesty's pleasure (i.e. without limit of time) for the unlawful killing of a two-year-old boy and condemned by the trial judge for 'unrivalled evil and barbarity'. Changes have taken place in the youth system, such as the setting-up of the Youth Justice Board, although for serious offences those above the age of ten remain ineluctably subject to the adult system of criminal justice.

The general belief among practitioners in the administration of the criminal process was that the case was hijacked by the media and by some politicians by exploiting natural public anxieties about the killing, and helped to preserve at present the youth justice policies towards serious offences. The criminal justice system for juveniles in England and Wales, based still on an age of legal (as opposed to social) responsibility of ten has been criticised universally, including by the UN Committee on Human Rights. Among Western European democracies this age of criminal responsibility is one of the lowest. Although both Venables and Thompson were initially released with new identities in 2001, Venables was recalled to prison in 2010 for being in possession of child pornography on his computer.

On 12 March 2013 the Magistrates' Association, which from the 1960s had supported the age of criminal responsibility at the existing age level, considered a recent resolution for review by government of the age of criminal responsibility. This questioning of the age of responsibility for juveniles whose offences have largely been adjudicated upon by the magistracy is significant. It emphasises a desire, by those judicially responsible in most cases for young offenders, for the process to be urgently reviewed.

This call for a review should form an integral part of the need for a Royal Commission on the Penal System. The future behaviour of the adolescent population aged ten-to-18 is an important aspect of the system for the 21st-century.

We would do well to recall the evidence of Sir Godfrey Lushington to the Gladstone Committee when he said that imprisonment of a young offender was a 125-year-old idea in which the unfavourable features of the idea of depriving a person of his liberty were inseparable from prison life.[8]

(d) NOMS (National Offender Management Service)

Of all the innovations of prison administration, since the creation of the Prison Commission following nationalisation in 1878 and the creation of the Prison Board in 1978, the establishment of NOMS in 2004 to merge the prison and probation services was the most significant innovation. It is timely to make any assessment of this important reorganization.

(e) Community Service

Community service orders (CSOs) began their life in January 1973 as a novel, distinctive penal sanction of a non-custodial variety. Even then the policy-makers and the penal administrators watered down the proposal that came from the sub-committee of the Advisory Council on the Penal System under Lady Wootton. As her biographer, Professor Ann Oakley, wrote in *A Critical Woman* in 2011,[9] she (Barbara Wootton) 'could imagine a world in which ineffective and humiliating indignities no longer happened … but it was the imagination she applied to a different aspect of penal policy, alternatives to prison, … that earned her a more enduring place in the history books'. Her committee's original proposal in the 1970 report was purely 'non-custody' — 'instead of sending people to prison it would be better to get them to do some useful work'. Punishment, she claimed, was ineffective. Less serious rather than more serious offences would be apt for CSOs; nothing more than reparative work in the community alongside non-offenders. Six pilot areas were selected by the Home Office and organized by

---

8. *Report of the Departmental Committee on Prisons 1895* (C. 7702) Minutes of Evidence Q. 11482, cited by the Advisory Council on the Penal System on *Young Adult Offenders* in 1974, paragraph 122, p 42.

9. London, Bloomsbury, 2011, p.272.

local Probation Services. This trials selection led to CSOs under the Criminal Justice Act 1972.

While the Probation and After-Care Service responded warmly to the proposal, administration after 1980 increasingly pooh-poohed the innovation, to the point where (in 2012) there was even a proposal to include in every sentence a 'punitive element' in every order similar to community work. The history of 40 years of diminution of the first penal innovation of probation at the beginning of the 20th-century deserves a thorough study.

Profit, in place of a sense of public service, has become the *leitmotif* of the penal system. Is this wise, and what are its wider ramifications?

(f) Parole

The discharge of prisoners from their time inside the custodial system is a topic of important debate and discussion. We think JUSTICE to be correct in its report *A New Parole System for England and Wales* (2009) in opting decisively for the establishment of an independent parole tribunal. The establishing of the Parole Board, under the provisions of the Criminal Justice Act 1967, was a significant innovation on an unlicensed practice of release by the Executive on licence. The board has not been officially reviewed since then, when it was a very different institution. Release of prisoners on various forms of licence had always existed, but it was at the discretion of the Home Secretary and largely limited to prisoners serving life sentences and juveniles detained during the Sovereign's pleasure. The principal exception was borstal training from which young offenders could be released on licence, which could be revoked for the outstanding period of a three year sentence. This function was performed by Local Review Committees at the establishment where the offender was detained. A similar system had applied to those serving sentences under the comparatively short-lived system of corrective training introduced by the Criminal Justice Act 1948 but abolished by the Criminal Justice Act 1967. Thus, until 1967, the paroling of prisoners was exclusively an act of executive government (the Home Secretary's power to release lifers on licence subject to recall was put on a statutory basis in section 57 of the

Criminal Justice Act 1948) and had no relevance to the substantive criminal law or to the practice and procedure of the criminal courts.

Originally, it was proposed that recommendations for parole would be made by the prison authorities; the Criminal Justice Act 1967 so provided. During its parliamentary passage, the Home Secretary (Roy Jenkins) was, however, persuaded to establish an independent review body to advise the Home Secretary, and to make recommendations. That basic approach persists to this day (subject to a change of government department), although the board has subsequently acquired some decision-making powers. What is perhaps significant is that Roy Jenkins was persuaded by certain penal reformers (among whom we can claim to be numbered) to establish the board with the provision that the chairman of the Parole Board should be a public figure who was not legally, let alone judicially, qualified. The first chairman (an inspired choice who proved to be outstanding) was Lord Hunt of Llanfair Waterdine (of Everest fame) and, with one or two notable exceptions, the chairmanship over 40 years has been held by public servants who were not lawyers. However, two recent chairmen of the board, Sir David Latham and Sir David Calvert-Smith, have both been retired senior judges (one a former Lord Justice of Appeal and the other a former High Court Judge) which indicates a tendency towards a judicial approach.

From its inception, the board has always contained three High Court judges, part-time, one of whom was invariably the vice-chairman of the board. A number of serving and retired Crown Court judges have also been part-time members, but the current membership of around 220 men and women is drawn from a range of disciplines. Thus the parole system became a mixed tribunal and a distinct part of the system of English administrative law.

At present the Parole Board is inundated with a backlog of applications for discharge from prisoners, exacerbated by the new system for allowing oral representations by the prisoner, after the former system was declared by the Supreme Court in the *Osborne* case in 2013 to be insufficiently fair. The 2014 discharge of Harry Roberts, after spending 48 years in custody for killing three police officers in 1966 (the tariff given at his trial was 30 years) is a good example of the need for a review of the discharge of prisoners.

The Prison and Public Policy

Seán McConville

I follow my distinguished colleagues in setting out something of the background that has led to a career-long interest in penal affairs. There was something immediately instructive and certainly symbolic in the fact that as an undergraduate on placement I first entered prison in the midst of the foot and mouth epidemic of the autumn of 1967. This was Leyhill, near Wotton-under-Edge, Gloucestershire, and the disinfectant trough was there for car tyres and footwear alike on passing from one physical, but I also came immediately to feel social, world into another. The transition and its meaning could easily be over-laboured, but in the near half-century that has followed I have sometimes reflected on it. Only a few feet of tarmac and an open gate separated the highway and the prison, but there were within that small area two very different worlds of expectations and preoccupations.

Since then I have studied, written and taught about the prison system in Britain, Europe and North America. As a member of a Board of Visitors (as the Independent Monitors used to be called) I inspected my local prison freely and at almost all hours. Consulting in prison litigation, I have been involved in prominent cases across the United States, Canada and Europe. With politicians, public administrators and prison managers I have pondered and debated the many problems and dilemmas of penal policy and management. Sometimes these discussions took on broad political and moral perplexities, sometimes they were confined to fairly narrow technical matters—even the minutiae of institutional life. On occasion claims about facts and their significance were strongly and lengthily contested in court. But always, framing the discussions, with varying degrees of explicitness, were basic questions about the purpose, usefulness and potentiality of penal action. And in the best of the exchanges there was acknowledgement that the curtailment of liberty is a grave responsibility, imposing heavy obligations of political and executive probity.

As a magistrate for some 16 years I had no doubt of the role of the prison as a component of a rational sentencing policy. Without the sanction of removal of liberty many less drastic penalties would not be workable; without the prison's emphatic and unambiguous statement of social disapproval, public confidence in criminal justice would falter. There are some commentators who would move away from custody altogether for swathes of offences but I do not think this is possible or even desirable. There are, sadly, more insidious and liberty-challenging ways of enforcing social order than prison gates. But having said this, the questions remain: who, why, for how long, in what conditions and why this rather than that?

During a decade of living and working in the United States I saw the prison and jail population double and witnessed a great public enthusiasm at least in theory for funding and building new institutions. Faced with the deeply troubling effects of illegal drugs and inner-city turmoil, politicians gave a commitment to build a way out of crime, through a rapidly expanding penal estate. But this was a reassuring, almost reflexive, commitment easily demanded by the public—especially in the wake of some frightening or revolting case, or worrying new trend—and almost as easy to give.

And who, seeking to obtain or hold on to public office, could be seen to be irresolute or to falter in this field? At some fairly early point, nevertheless, the promises and public acquiescence had to be tested in the everyday world of fiscal choices. Neither party to the bargain entered into it in good faith, or really wanted to deliver: this was complicity in wishfulness. In default, attempts were inevitably made to squeeze more men and women prisoners into insufficient and inadequate accommodation. But this was only the beginning. Inflated demand for bed-spaces without the matching supply of funding and resources meant that one had to have many of the prisoners live without a proper and proportionate supply of civilising and indeed essential services such as mental and physical medical care, or education; or to have men and women many of whom were of a violent and deeply disturbed character crowded together without safe and proper correctional supervision; to allow premises to deteriorate for lack of maintenance; to feed poor diets; to pay little regard to family and community ties and employment prospects—and so on. These were the wholly predictable consequences of a panic-driven agenda. And at some point almost all those who had lived for years in such conditions returned, largely unprepared and negatively socialised, to the challenges of freedom.

Some but by no means all of these and many other often quite shocking derelictions and instances of short-sighted disregard—unhappily relished and brandished about as talismans of credibility by a minority of irresponsible office-seekers—came into conflict with basic civil and human standards guaranteed by the constitutions of the individual states and the Union (in Canada the Charter). Courts are backstops in these circumstances and can never be efficient administrators, but if the legislative branch falters in its obligations the judicial one must step in. The result of this collision of branches of government was often in response to court-ordered remedies, a rash of *trompe-l'oeil* contrivances—accelerated release, periodic amnesties, selective incapacitation, plea-bargaining, and so-called back-door, side-door and trap-door schemes for concealing releases without embarrassing the executive. But the prison population continued to rise inexorably and with it more spending and administrative muddle.

From these years of work and observation I drew a number of conclusions. Some of these were fairly obvious, such as the contradiction between the sometimes supremely confident statement of policy and its truly haphazard, ill-considered and uncoordinated nature. (Indeed the relationship between the two sides of that equation is almost invariably strong). I also came to understand how very difficult it can be in a modern democracy for politicians to handle these matters rationally and indeed as many of them would wish. These observations brought me back to a theme and a seemingly perennial problem that I had encountered many years before when serving as a House of Commons specialist advisor to the Expenditure and then the Home Affairs Committee, as well as the Council of Europe: how most profitably might we approach the construction of durable, efficient and humane penal policies?

Making Penal Policy

There have been years of crisis for many of the institutions that support our society. Child abuse perpetrated under institutional cover, or in the community, and ignored for reasons of political convenience and appalling misjudgement of social priorities have shocked us all. Financial institutions have behaved with self-serving recklessness and large commercial enterprises have stubbornly engaged in deeply-unethical small-print dealings and sleight of hand with their customers. Services once deeply-trusted such as the police and portions of the caring professions have failed to live up to their declarations and our expectations. And for garnishing we have of course the political class—the petty corruption in the last Parliament casts a long shadow. Of the occupations that contribute to the public good that of politician is among the more important: damage here can be damage everywhere.

But because we have crises we should not assume that public life is in crisis. We continue to run a free country in a decent and humane way, to wrestle with conflicting demands, interests and priorities in usually civilised and respectful debate. We collect and use information fairly effectively and—importantly—we generally do not seek to blackguard those with whom we disagree. Politicians in their trade must combine principle with deviousness and opportunism, practise the arts of timing as well as the virtues of constancy. In the making of public policy therefore there must be a persistence of manoeuvre—the advancement of one's party or oneself as well as the public good. When these latter elements all fall into line (and they surprisingly often do so) policy can be constructed or modified with minimum friction and maximum advantage. The tumult and rough and tumble of the day should not obscure most politicians' desire to give public service and to see successful outcomes.

All areas of public policy and the allocation of resources are prone to disagreement—sometimes vigorously so. Quite apart from matters which are so technical that the decisions are made according to relatively objective criteria, research findings and measurements, there will always be debate of varying degrees of intensity: no democracy could wish it otherwise. There are however some topics which are particularly prone to inflammatory and accusatory exchanges and where public anxiety may be fanned as part of the exchange, to win advantage. Health, social security policy and penal affairs fall within this group.

How we deal with the offender is always a vexing and frequently baffling matter and, with much of the intellectual history of the last century and more, has been cast in the nature/nurture, free-choice/social influence mould. We can rarely reach agreement about the causes of crime and the weight that should attach to social and structural as against individual and temperamental factors, and indeed whether there are 'individual factors' as distinct from a combination of external influences. This leads on to a consideration of culpability and that in turn to social and penal action. Turning to offences, we find it hard to compare the gravity of different kinds of crime, although we believe that we can more easily calculate gravity within an offence category. How, for example to compare the manufacture and sale of illegal substances with robbery or environmental pollution; or misrepresentation in trade with social security fraud? Combining our assessment of the offender and the offence we find ourselves in calculations of some complexity, both in relation to degree of harm and opprobrium and to moral agency and responsibility.

As ordinary citizens these are difficult enough matters to process, and certainly not easier for politicians debating and making laws. Tradition and convention assist to some considerable extent to help us find agreements, but times change and public sentiments drift. Add the extreme cases that inevitably feature in the news media and one gets spates of volatility. It is hard to blame journalists and their editors for picking up the hard case — a great part of their *raison d'etre* and daily task is to capture the readers', listeners' or viewers' attention. The difficulty is that public opinion then tends to be influenced, sometimes formed, by the hard and unusual rather than the usual and banal crimes which tend to be nuisances and a depressing drain rather than threats. Crime moreover is easily understood as an incident — most of us at some point will have been the victim of a theft, deception, unpleasant and possibly unlawful verbal exchange, or will know someone who has been. And in virtually all communities serious crimes have taken place at some point and have stamped themselves on the public consciousness, however eased by the passage of time.

The Political Process

Politics depend on contest. The quest for office gives energy and tests ideas. The competition acts as a rough kind of assessment if not of fitness then of survival and of character. Individual politicians compete for places within their parties and parties compete for public influence and votes. It is a commonplace that modes of involvement in politics have changed greatly in the last two decades. By no means all but a much larger proportion of those who now go into politics do so as a career which is planned from early adulthood. Political societies at college or university, passing on to local government or the central offices of political parties, appointment as special advisors or researchers for MPs and Ministers, or posts in politically aligned think-tanks—and thence to safe seats via the rite of the unwinnable one (or two). This is not the place to ponder the virtues and drawbacks of such a system, but we may observe that it brings together with special intensity the personal and the political: the fate of the party and its professional politician fuse to a remarkable degree. Loss of employment and fracture of career can follow political failure. This in turn makes for a special and intimate interest in elections and re-election prospects. It has always been so, perhaps, but surely not with such intensity.

In these circumstances, and with all the new and sophisticated psephological methods of assessing—indeed minutely dissecting—the temper and passing tides of public opinion it is inevitable an acute sensitivity to electoral shifts and tremors will significantly influence the formation and promulgation of policy. Timelines, moreover, are condensed: winning an election and then immediately turning to the prospects and preparation for the next is now the pattern of political life. MPs want a party leadership which above all will put them into or help retain office or their parliamentary career. It would be cynical and shallow to say that this is for purely personal reasons. People are active in political parties because they support their general approach on such issues as income distribution, social equality and amelioration, defence and foreign policy and all the related and subsidiary policies. To a considerable degree (which the parties are usually embarrassed to acknowledge) there is an overlap in thinking and priorities. The book-keeping constraints of tax-take, structural deficit, demography and demand for public services severely reduce the discretional element in decision-making. Language and presentation become important in claiming distinctions and asserting competence and sincerity over one's opponent. Criminal and penal policy are especially apt for this type of hoof-drumming and horn-locking. It becomes very hard in these circumstances for any active political leader to curb dramatic opinion, even if it is of only approximate accuracy. Behind him or her the ranks will want to know why an opportunity has been missed to show strength or to deal a blow to the credibility of the other side. Considering what is best for the public good in the medium or long term is all but impossible.

A Royal Commission

Our contention—and it is based on several decades of observation and engagement—is that the political mechanism is ill-adapted to construct and promulgate penal and related criminal justice policy. The outcomes are simply perverse. Between 1992 and 2013 the incarceration rate in England and Wales has risen from 90 prisoners per 100,000 of population to 148 per 100,000.[1] This population increase has almost entirely been based on sentenced prisoners (as distinct from remands in custody). Remarkably this absolute and proportionate increase has taken place against the background of falling crime. The Crime Survey for England and Wales is widely agreed to be the most reliable measure of crimes actually occurring (as distinct, for example, from those reported to and recorded by the police). In 2012, the survey estimated that the eight million criminal incidents that took place was less than half of those of 1995. Courts have become more likely to sentence to imprisonment in the disposal of cases and those custodial sentences have become longer. The prison population is also becoming 'heavier' in another way, with the proportion of those serving indeterminate life sentences rising from 8 per cent of the prison population in 1992 to 19 per cent in 2012. The number of those serving life-sentences has increased from around 3,000 in 1992 to almost 14,000. There are few economies of scale and imprisonment remains expensive, with places annually costing somewhere between £35,000 and £40,000 per person.

We have here a disjunction that were it to occur in almost any other field of public administration would have been at the centre of a prolonged national debate.

---

1.   These and other figures and trends have been usefully and instructively brought together in the British Academy's (July, 2014) report: *A Presumption Against Imprisonment: Social Order and Social Values* (London: The British Academy). We draw on this authoritative report for the statistics that follow. For this incarceration rate see pp.29-30. The incarceration rate for England and Wales is significantly higher than for comparable European countries such as Germany and Sweden.

Expenditure is being incurred on a vast scale, proportionately out of line with our comparable neighbours in Europe, and at a time when there is a decline rather than an increase in crime. Politicians are not malign, neither are they lacking in intelligence. It may be an observation against the grain of the times, but it is impossible to believe that those in mainstream public life wish their country ill. The only conclusion therefore is that we have in penal and related criminal policy issues that cannot now be handled in a wholly rational way, that here the ornamental and competitive elements in political life overshadow the pragmatic and empirical. This has not always been the case, but it is no part of our argument here to bemoan the loss of what always must be a slightly doubtful 'golden age' of bi-partisanship in penal and criminal policy, or to attempt to analyse the reasons for the shift.

If the reader concedes any substance in the case so far there is an inevitable question: how do we move away from the present system of policy-making? The problem is not an easy one for, as we have observed, penal and criminal policy statements are politically powerful and no party leadership is going to give them up. There thus is a stand-off: Party A will not move to some kind of bi-partisanship, or enter into a self-denying ordinance, until Party B does — and then, what if A or B reneges? There is also the organic pressure to which we have alluded and a reluctance to abandon electoral ammunition: not everyone is representing a safe seat. We think the only way to go beyond this state of policy paralysis is to appoint a Royal Commission.

The Commission at Work

The Thatcher administration saw in the advisory bodies — the so-called quangos — several undesirable elements of the post-war consensus which it believed was at least in part to blame for the decline of the nation. It discerned in these bodies an implied agreement not to see, never mind to ask, the difficult questions, and to skirt around potentially divisive social issues — to fudge. These were also bodies in which patronage was exercised for the benefit of approved persons of centrist and 'insider' views and beliefs. The quangos would therefore veil rather than illuminate and would certainly block critical and socially radical opinion. They were also, the Thatcher government thought, expensive means of delaying decisions that urgently had to be taken, of kicking issues out of contention into the long grass. The conclusion to this line of thinking was inescapable: if advice were needed let Ministers commission it, setting the remit and a time-scale for response.

Many will not like or agree with this characterisation of the quango culture, but others will recognise that Margaret Thatcher and her administration had some merit on their side when they sought to create a stronger and more directly accountable decision-making process and to sweep away what they saw as risk-averse woolliness. Why then would we wish to return to an outdated format and method of work in appointing a Royal Commission? Surely there are recent and compelling negative examples of the incorrigible defects of these big enquiries? The Saville Inquiry into the events of Bloody Sunday took some 12 years and much treasure to complete. The Chilcot Inquiry into events surrounding the Iraq War, announced in June 2009, has still to report, and doubtless will also come with a hefty bill. Why therefore set up another of these delay-making and potentially inconclusive talking-shops?

The elements for a successful inquiry are well-known and there is every reason to apply them to a Royal Commission on the Penal System. Tight terms of reference and an experienced chair and secretariat are a *sine qua non*, but so also is a fixed timetable for completion. We think that the work we have in mind could and ought to be completed within two years, from the appointment of members to the publication of the report.[2] This condition would be emphasised and the submission date would not be negotiable. The report would be what could be done within the allotted period and no extension would be contemplated or authorised. Verbal evidence, which sometimes is mere grandstanding and often is of poor quality, of doubtful relevance and hard to use, would be restricted to an

---

2.   The timing is not plucked out of the air. Assuming that the Commission were appointed in the opening months of a new Parliament (which we now know to be fixed-term) the report would be submitted about half-way through the session. Were it left much longer than that the party divisions arising from electoral preparations would prevent anything approaching a dispassionate reception for the Commission's recommendations. We calculate that a report could be prepared and debated within this 'close season' and at least a start made on implementation.

absolute minimum, and that almost invariably the testing of the most important and cogent written submissions. The secretariat should be strong, widely and competitively recruited, and with duties extending well beyond the enabling and clerical often provided on these occasions. It should be a small body of experts and practical fact finders, well-led and amply supported, able to find and marshal data and actively to engage in the dynamics of the enquiry with the commissioners. In these days of excellent data storage and easy retrieval there is little need for domestic visits of inspection, much less overseas trips. Instead, there should be invited to make submissions to the Commission those who have unquestionable expertise and a case to present or flaws to expose: the usual assembly of one-stringed instruments is a mere impediment. With this focused and sensible business-like style of proceeding a substantial body of material could be reviewed and worked into an integrated report within a two-year period.

The function of the inquiry would be to set the direction of penal policy for a generation or more. To do this it would need to take a broad approach. This would not take us into generalities, although that danger—and generalisations are always easy and seductive—would have to be guarded against. In the light of all we have argued so far it should be clear that a Commission would have to rise above ideological and political differences in approaching penal affairs; it should free politicians and other policy-makers from the yoke of their occupational obligations and prior positions. The Commission would aim to mark out a field and to provide rules that would allow a rational approach to policy that would exclude zero-sum and finger-pointing temptations. We do not for a moment believe that a species of universal harmony would be established, and that there would in consequence be a consensus in all penal policy. These are difficult moral and empirical issues and men and women of good faith will always—should always—differ on them. But if the haphazard accretions of successive waves of partisan policy-making could be put to one side and if evidence based options could be set out, and impossible expectations put to rest, there is a good chance—far better than we now have—of adopting, testing and evaluating penal methods and making the bigger, more responsible and productive choices.

The Questions

The setting of the remit for the Royal Commission would itself involve a process of public consultation, followed by discussion and Ministerial decision. We have a short list but recognise that this is but a start of the conversation that would launch the inquiry.

What is the relationship between crime rates and punishment in the United Kingdom?

Given a finite budget for the penal system how best should it be spent?

What should the public reasonably expect of the penal system?

Outside the formal justice system are there reliable means of dealing with offending?

How should criminal justice research evaluate and inform policy?

About the authors

Louis Blom-Cooper QC appeared in many high-profile cases, including at the Old Bailey and in (what is now) the Supreme Court. He taught criminology and penology at Bedford College, University of London, holds several honorary doctorates and is a fellow of King's College, London. His books include *Fine, Lines and Distinctions: Murder, Manslaughter and the Taking of Human Life* (with the late Terence Morris) (Waterside Press, 2011). Prominent in the campaign for the abolition of the death penalty, he was a founder member of the Prison Reform Trust and of the Homicide Review Advisory Group (HOMRAG).

Seán McConville is Professor of Law and Public Policy at Queen Mary, University of London. He has published widely on law, politics, imprisonment and penal affairs and has taught, researched and advised legislatures, governments and advisory bodies on both sides of the Atlantic. During a ten-year residence in the USA he took part in high-profile prison litigation in several states. His book, *Irish Political Prisoners 1920-1962: Pilgrimage of Desolation War* (Routledge, 2013), continues his study of politically-motivated offenders. At the end of this multi-year research and writing programme, the final volume of his 'Irish trilogy' will bring his account of Irish political prisoners and their part in Irish politics and Anglo-Irish relations up to the Good Friday Agreement.

The author of the Foreword

Sir Henry Brooke CMG was a High Court Judge for eight years, and a Lord Justice Appeal for a further ten, before he retired in 2006. He is a former Chairman of the Law Commission, and between 1997 and 2001 was chairman of the Centre for Crime and Justice Studies. He was the judge in charge of the modernisation of the English law courts from 2001 to 2004.

Appendix I: Reports

a. Reports by the Advisory Council for the Treatment of Offenders (ACTO) (1944-1964)

1. Proposal that a Special Institution Outside the Prisons should be Provided for Offenders with Abnormal Mental Characteristics (1944)
2. Report on Dartmoor Prison by Mr George Benson MP
3. Suspended Sentences (1952)
4. Alternatives to Short Terms of Imprisonment (1957)
5. The After-care and Supervision of Discharged Prisoners (1958)
6. The Treatment of Young Offenders (1958)
7. Capital Punishment Cmnd 1213 (1960)
8. Non-Residential Treatment of Offenders under 21 (1962)
9. Preventive Detention (1963)
10. The Organisation of After-Care (1963).

b. Reports by the Advisory Council on the Penal System (ACPS) (1966-1978)

1. Interim Report on Detention of Girls in a Detention Centre (1968)
2. The Regime for Long-Term Prisoners in Conditions of Maximum Security (1968)
3. Detention Centres (1970)
4. Non-Custodial and Semi-Custodial Penalties (1970)
5. Reparation by the Offender (1970)
6. Young Adult Offenders (1974)
7. Powers of the Courts Dependent on Imprisonment (1977)
8. The Length of Prison Sentences (1977)
9. Sentences of Imprisonment (1978).

Appendix II: Letters to the Press

1. **Letter to *The Times*, published 10 April 1995 under the title 'Time to review prisons policy'.[1]**

Sir, Tomorrow, April 10, marks the centenary of the submission to Home Secretary Herbert Asquith of the Gladstone Committee's Report on Prisons. This committee propagated the twin philosophies of deterrence and rehabilitation, which greatly influenced penal affairs for much of the 20th century. In recent years, however, both the question of rehabilitation and the issue of deterrence have become highly problematic, as has their relationship. The use of punishment by society needs careful consideration, as does the value of imprisonment.

The present state of our prison system, as chronicled in the penetrating reports of HM Chief Inspector of Prisons, Judge Stephen Tumim, is such as to cause confusion in the minds of many members of the public, and even in the Prison Service itself. The valuable recommendations of the 1990-91 inquiry into prison disturbances by Lord (then Lord Justice) Woolf proposed a civilised regime for prisons, and justice for prisoners, but these objectives have now, to some extent, been overtaken by other agendas.

Lord Woolf's inquiry, moreover, did not have the remit to relate its findings to sentencing policy and practice. We think the time is ripe for an overview, on the scale of the Gladstone inquiry, to propound a sound and authoritative penal philosophy for the 21st century.

Yours faithfully,

Seán McConville (Professor of Law and Public Policy, Queen Mary, University of London)
Lord Allen of Abbeydale (Permanent Under Secretary, Home Office, 1966-72)

---

1. The letters in this *Appendix* are reproduced by kind consent of *The Times* and *Guardian* respectively.

Louis Blom-Cooper (Member, Home Secretary's Advisory Council on the Penal System, 1966-78)

Anthony E Bottoms (Wolfson Professor of Criminology, University of Cambridge, 1984-2006)

James Callaghan (Home Secretary, 1967-70, later Lord Callaghan of Cardiff)

Ralph Gibson (Lord Justice of Appeal, 1985-94)

John K Harding (Chief Probation Officer, Inner London, 1993-2001)

John Hunt (Chairman, Parole Board for England and Wales, 1967-74)

Terence Morris (Professor Emeritus, Criminology and Criminal Justice, University of London)

Brendan O'Friel (Chairman, Prison Governors' Association, 1977-95)

Lord Runcie (Archbishop of Canterbury, 1980-91)

2. Letter to *The Times*, published 3 June 1996 under the title 'Penal philosophy for 21st century'.

Sir, On April 10, 1995, you published a letter from us marking the centenary of the report of the Gladstone Committee on Prisons, urging an overview on the scale of the Gladstone inquiry, 'to propound a sound and authoritative penal philosophy for the 21st century' — in short, a royal commission on crime and punishment. Little, if any, political attention was paid then or since, either to the centenary or to the proposal for an inquiry.

In the intervening period, however, events have repeatedly emphasised the need for an authoritative and deliberate review of our criminal justice and penal systems. An unprecedented, publicly conducted argument between the Home Office and the higher judiciary over sentencing policy has gone on unabated.

On May 23 the retiring Lord Chief Justice, Lord Taylor of Gosforth, initiated a Lords debate on government proposals, as outlined in the White Paper, *Protecting the Public*. In his recent speech to the Prison Reform Trust the Archbishop of Canterbury, speaking with great moral authority and drawing on extensive pastoral experience of the prisons, emphasised the need for a proper balance within the penal system between the various purposes of punishment.

In a pre-election period there must now be grave concern that consideration of criminal and penal policy will stray even further from the course recommended by the Archbishop. Over the last two decades the United States has shown the tragic and counter-productive results of mixing competitive party politics with such policy debates and thereby inflaming public prejudice. This is a field where the national interest demands that bipartisanship should be striven for, even while legitimate party differences are debated.

It is essential to safeguard criminal and penal policy from such dangers, by providing a mechanism to address these important issues, dispassionately, authoritatively and constructively. It is time for a royal commission.

Yours faithfully,

(Signatories as for the letter of 10 April 1995, absent James Callaghan)

3. Letter to *The Times*, published 25 October 2005 under the title 'Ten years on, the politics of penal reform are as short-sighted as ever'.

Sir, More than a decade ago you published a letter (April 10, 1995) with 11 signatures calling for an independent commission on criminal justice and the penal system. That date marked the centenary of the submission to Home Secretary Herbert Asquith of the Gladstone Committee's Report on Prisons, which set out the broad course of penal policy for the 20th century.

The letter deplored the fragmentation of penal policy and its consequent erratic and uneven course and said that the present state of our prison system is such as to cause confusion in the minds of many members of the public, and even in the Prison Service itself. This, sadly, has continued.

Both Conservative and Labour administrations have made excessive room for party political considerations. All too clearly this year's party conference season confirmed that this will persist. Short-term initiatives, imbalances, the pursuit of contradictory objectives and over-ambitious promises are thus inevitable.

Cynicism swells, politicians seek to placate it, and the vicious spiral continues.

Our prisons epitomise much of this. Nothing in the last decade has curbed overcrowding. Large investments notwithstanding, numbers teeter on the very edge of operating capacity. Overcrowding nullifies rehabilitative programmes and crushes the spirit of staff and prisoners alike. Reconviction rates have scarcely budged and the same dismal stage army of offenders trudges expensively through courts, probation offices and penal institutions.

The case for an authoritative overview is more pressing than ever. A Royal Commission could, for a generation or more, provide the framework for a set of sound and realistic criminal and penal policies; it would simultaneously free politicians from their counterproductive strife in this sensitive field.

In all areas of public policy there will be disagreement over balance, detail and style. But is it too much to hope that the way to a higher consensus on criminal and penal philosophy for the 21st century can be found?

Yours faithfully,

Seán McConville [as above]
Lord Allen of Abbeydale [as above]
Sir Louis Blom-Cooper QC [as above]
Sir Anthony E Bottoms [as above]
Charles Bushell (General Secretary of the Prison Governors' Association 2003-2007)
John K Harding [as above]
Lord Hurd of Westwell (Home Secretary, 1985-89)
Ian Loader (Professor of Criminology, University of Oxford, 2005-)
Terence Morris [as above]
Martin Narey (Director-General, HM Prison Service, 1999-2003)
Lord Woolf (Lord Chief Justice of England and Wales, 2000-2005)

4. Letter to the *Guardian*, published 16 June 2006 under the title 'Call an enquiry into the criminal justice system'.

The dissection of the current panic over crime and prisons (Amid this panic over stabbings, we are ignoring what really cuts crime, June 9) is compelling reading for all concerned with the administration of justice. Polly Toynbee's article demands from ministers a response that calmly and realistically reflects on the state of our criminal justice system and offers some hope for the 139 prisons that are bursting at the seams. Nothing less than an authoritative independent commission will help us regain a grip on criminal and penal policy and public confidence. A commission of full-time members should now be appointed, given the resources to complete the work and directed to report within 18 months.

Prof Sean McConville
Louis Blom-Cooper QC
Queen Mary, University of London

www.ingramcontent.com/pod-product-compliance
Lightning Source LLC
Chambersburg PA
CBHW081508290326
41933CB00045B/3150